STARTERS
LONG AGO
BOOKS

The
Sun People

Macdonald Educational

temple

These men played a ball game long ago.
They called it pok-a-tok.
They played it in courts in front of the temple.
They played it for the gods.

stone ring

Pok-a-tok was played in Mexico,
in South America.
The Maya and the Aztecs played it.

This ball game player worships
the Maya sun god.
The Aztecs and the Incas had sun gods too.
So we often call them the sun people.
They all lived in South America.

4

The sun people had many other gods.
Here is the rain god.
Rain is falling from his hands.

crocodile

The Maya had many parades.
They wore special headdresses.
The headdresses looked like animals.
One man wore a crocodile.

6

This is the Maya Chief.
He wore animal clothes too.
His servants dressed him for the parade.
They put on his jewels and decorated his skin.

7

a Maya observatory

inside the observatory

sun slits

Here is a Maya observatory.
Astronomers went there to watch the sun.
As the sun moved across the sky,
it sometimes shone through slits
into the observatory.
8

a Maya calendar

month signs

POP   YAXKIN   MAC   ZIO   MUAN

The sun helped Maya astronomers
to make calendars.
One calendar counted days.
Another calendar showed the months.
The picture shows some of its month signs.

This picture is from a folding book.
It tells the story of prince Eight-Deer.
The picture shows him with his friend Four-Tiger.
They are sailing to attack a town.

10

This is another page from the book.
The story is told in pictures.
The sun people had no alphabet.
They could not write words.
So they used pictures instead of words.

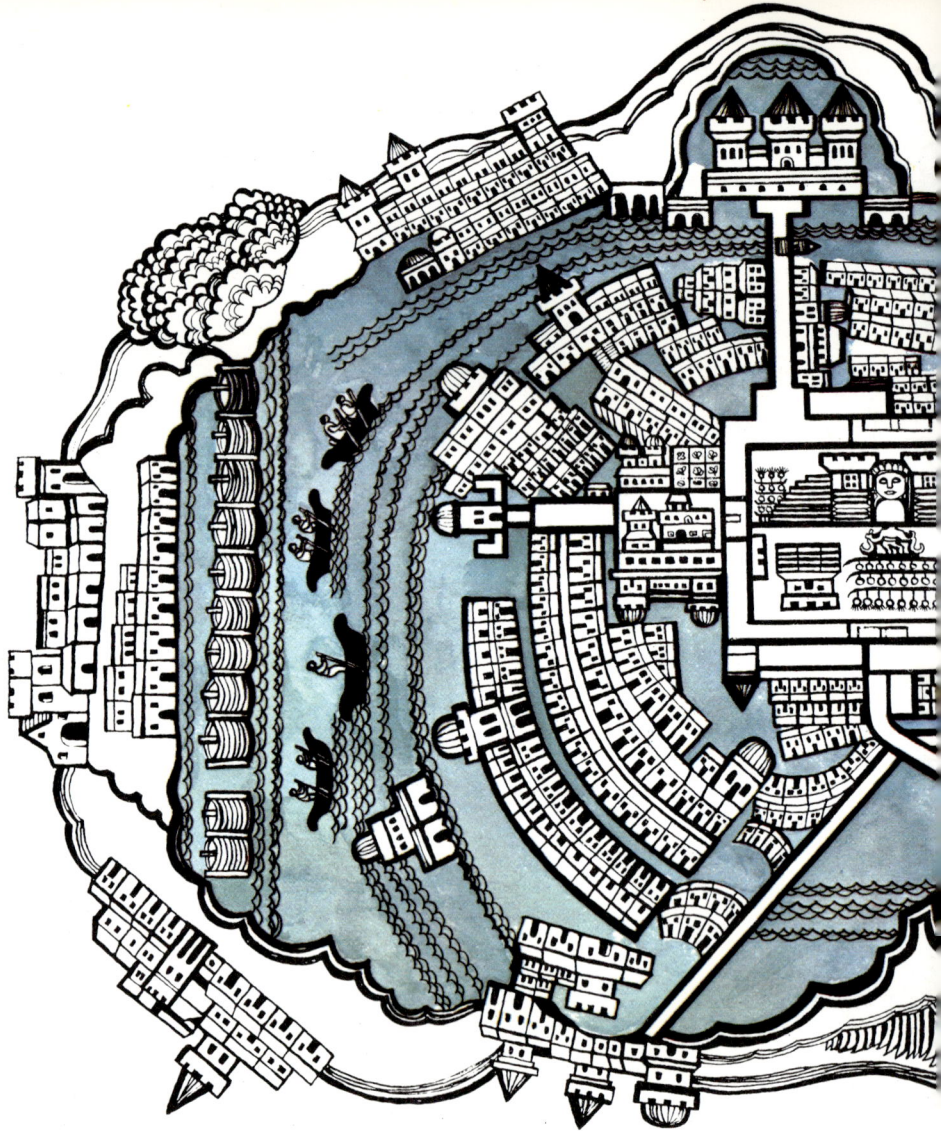

Here is the map of an Aztec city.
The city was called Tenochtitlan.
Cortes, a Spaniard, drew a map like this
when he captured the city.

12

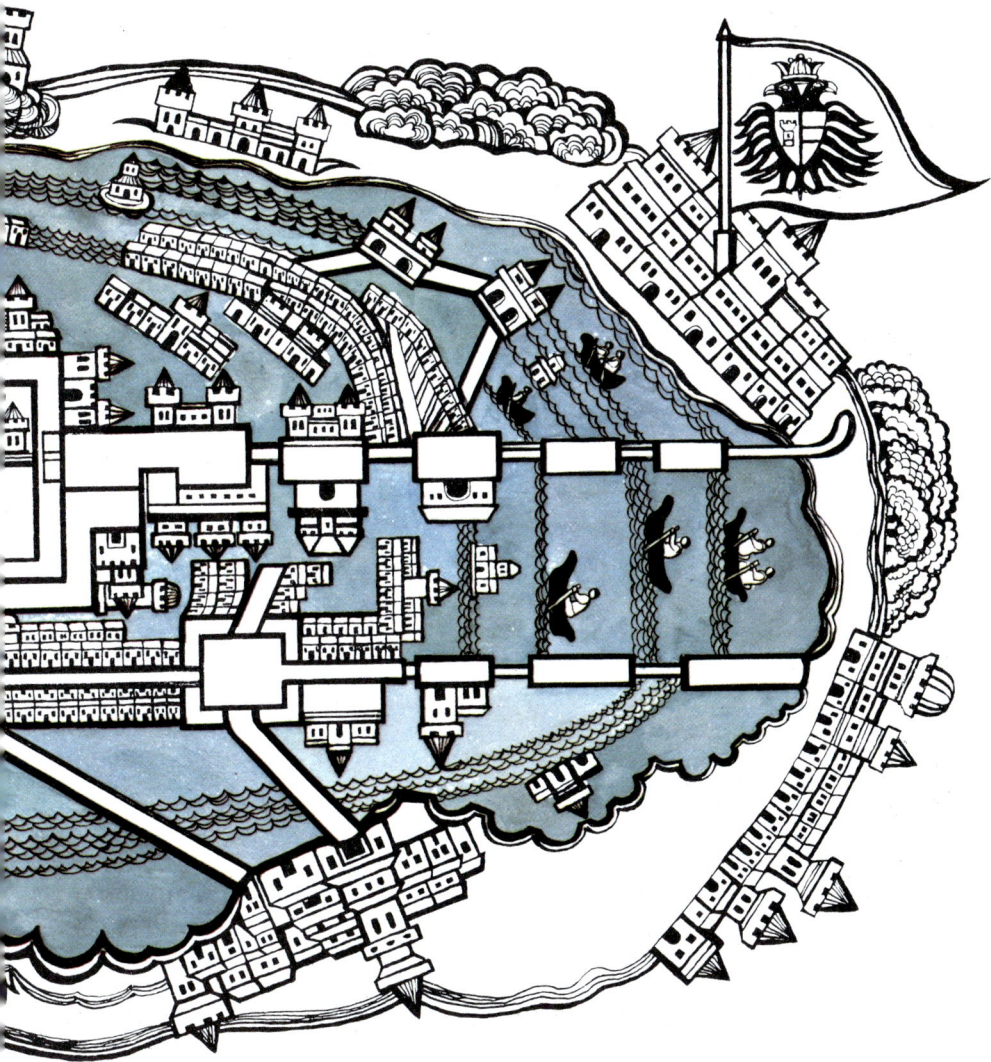

The city was built on an island in a lake.
It had temples and palaces
and gardens of flowers.
Rivers ran along some streets.
So people travelled in boats.

pottery market

carrier

This is a busy Maya village.
Some people are buying pots
in the market.
Others ride canoes on the river.

carriers

potter

fish seller

There are some carriers carrying packs.
The packs are full of things to sell.
The men are taking them
to sell in another village.

15

1. Melting the gold ore.

2. Refining the gold.

3. Making gold blocks.

4. Beating the gold into plates.

The Incas made many things out of gold.
They dug the gold from the ground.
The pictures show how the gold workers
made their treasures.

Here is the handle of an Inca knife.
It is made of gold and jewels.
It is made in the shape of a god.

loom

The Incas made beautiful cloth.
Here are some weavers in a cloth factory.
They are weaving the cloth on looms.
Everyone weaves a different pattern.

This Inca cloth was made in wool.
It has a pattern in many colours.

These Inca carriers are going to market.
The market is on the other side of the river.
The men cross the river on a bridge of rope.
The bridge was called the San Luis Rey.

rope bridge

The bridge is high above the river.
It hangs between towers on each side.
The bridge swings as the men walk on it.

1. sowing maize

2. guarding the crop

3. gathering the crop.

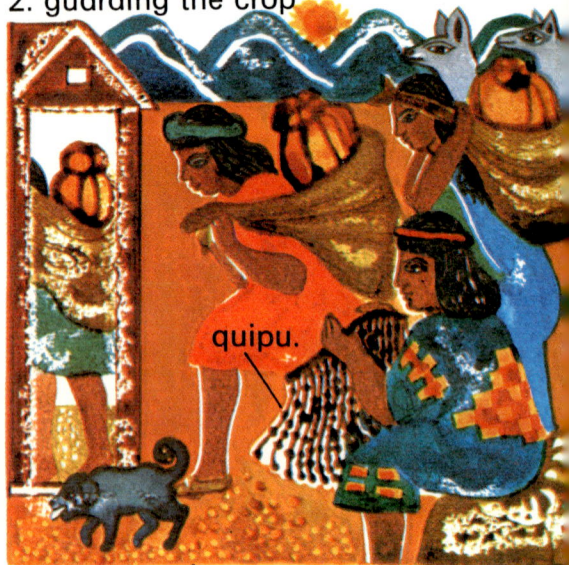
quipu.

4. counting the crop with a quipu.

The sun people all grew maize for food.
The pictures show an Inca farmer growing maize.
The maize cobs were stored in a barn.
The farmer counted them on a quipu.

22

Maize was an important food.
So the sun people prayed to the maize god.

town gate

town walls

guards

Cuzco was the capital city of the Incas.
Many people visited it.
The Inca kings lived in Cuzco.

24

parasol

sedan chair

Here is a king in a procession.
He was the last Inca king.
Spaniards captured his kingdom.
The sun kingdoms ended
when the Spaniards came.

card

Sellotape   paints

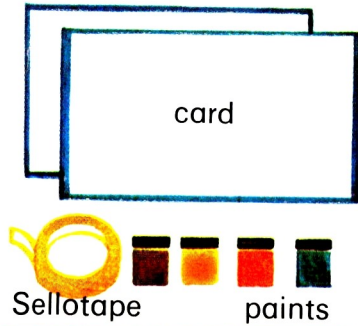

1. Paint an animal on the card.

3. You could add
   your own decorations.

2. Sellotape the cards together at each end.

See if you can make an animal headdress,
like the ones the Mayans wore.
Make it from paper or card.

paints

Cut potatoes in half.
Cut patterns in the potatoes, like this.

Try printing an Inca pattern.
You can use potatoes.
Dip the potato shapes in paint.
Press them onto paper or cloth.

Index